The Dragon Within

Also by this author

Self-help
Mother, Lover, Woman, Warrior

Middle Grade Fiction
The Day the Colours Went Away

Children's Fiction
Waiting for Sanjay

KILEY BAKER

THE DRAGON WITHIN

Poetry for the not-faint-of-heart.

First published by Busybird Publishing 2025

Copyright © 2025 Kiley Baker

ISBN:
Hardcover: 978-1-923501-06-5
Paperback: 978-1-923501-07-2
Ebook: 978-1-923501-08-9

This book is copyright. Apart from any fair dealing for the purposes of study, research, criticism, review, or as otherwise permitted under the Copyright Act, no part may be reproduced by any process without written permission. Enquiries should be made through the publisher.

This is a work of fiction. Any similarities between places and characters are a coincidence.

Cover image: ID 300483483 © Retrosesos | Dreamstime.com

Other images used: longing: ID 356939029 © Oleksandr Bykov Dreamstime.com
Secrets: ID 367142130 © Alla Parhomenko Dreamstime.com
Reclamation: ID 262418943 © Antonios Karvelas Dreamstime.com
grey smoke: ID 28170287 © William Langeveld | Dreamstime.com

Cover design: Kiley Baker

Layout and typesetting: Busybird Publishing

Busybird Publishing
2/118 Para Road
Montmorency, Victoria
Australia 3094
www.busybird.com.au

*This collection of poems is dedicated to the dreamers and the empaths.
For those that feel so much but speak too little.
To those at the start and those in the middle.
It's also for those at the end looking backward
remembering how far they've come.
It's also mainly for the old me.
Well done, little one.*

Reading this collection of poems feels like being invited into the sacred, unguarded corners of the author's soul. With astonishing honesty and unwavering courage, Kiley lays bare her inner world—her desires, wounds, triumphs, and truths—turning raw emotion into poetry that cuts straight to the heart.

What sets this collection apart is Kiley's remarkable precision with language. Each word feels intentionally placed, chosen with the care of someone who knows that true healing begins when we can finally name what hurts. Her ability to describe her innermost feelings with such clarity creates not just imagery, but emotional presence—her pain, joy, rage, and tenderness become almost tangible. You don't just read Kiley's poems; you feel them.

This is more than poetry—it's a journey of self-discovery and transformation. Central to Kiley's work is the hard-won realization that self-worth isn't found in others, but in the act of forgiving, accepting, and loving oneself. Through battles both internal and external, she emerges not unscathed, but authentic—and that's her power.

This collection is a testament to what happens when someone writes without flinching, when they choose truth over comfort and healing over hiding. It's as brave as it is beautiful. I am deeply moved and grateful to have witnessed this journey through her words.

Mgr Marcela Hackett.
Masters in English and French Philology,
graduating from Palacky University in Olomouc,
Czech Republic in 1998.

Contents

Longing   1

    Daddy's Girl   3

    Missing Champion   5

    It's You   7

    The Game   9

    The Sometimes Girl   11

    I Miss You   13

    Seductive Steel   15

    The Wrong Idea   17

    Regretful   19

    Thinking of You   21

    Only the Walls   23

    Apologetic   25

    At Arm's Length   27

    If I Were Pretty   29

    Smo   31

    In Memory: Daniel Fox   33

    Selfie   35

    Your Pretty Eyes   37

    Realisation   39

    For Marshall   41

Secrets — 47

- Insomnia — 49
- Little Too Late — 51
- Social Anxiety — 53
- You Had to Know — 55
- Submission — 57
- Does She Know? — 61
- Black Angel — 63
- Drunk — 65
- Crawling — 67
- Matriarchy — 69
- 2015 — 71
- To the Bone — 73
- Amanda — 75

Reclamation — 77

- Liar Liar — 79
- Fighting — 81
- The Dojo — 83
- The Dragon Within — 85
- Namaste — 87
- Let it Fall — 89
- What If? — 91
- Out of Shadow — 93
- Cracks — 95
- Spinning Cranes — 97
- Forgive Me — 99
- If — 101
- Never Give Up — 103
- The Mighty Queen — 105
- Ode to a New Year — 107
- Obsidian — 109
- Acknowledgements — 111
- About the Author — 113

Longing

Daddy's Girl

I've been many things to men,
but never Daddy's girl.

Yes, I confess, I've lifted my dress
to undeserving males,
hoping they see a pretty damsel,
forlorn and in distress,
needing rescuing like all the fairy tales,
but I've never been Daddy's princess.

I will admit to mothering some—
the shopping, the laundry, the cooking.
Playing the role of attentive housewife,
yet still sexy and fun,
dressing well and always good-looking,
but I've never been Daddy's little one.

I've melted the chocolate and drunk the wine,
performed a sensual dance.
I've pushed down longing to just be me,
pretending I'm just fine
as a sexy one-nighter, not a romance,
but I've never been Daddy's little sunshine.

I've waited and waited for 'til death do us part,
somewhere becoming a mother.
I have tried to forgive infidelity,
thinking over we could start,
but I could never escape the vision of another…
No, I've never been Daddy's sweetheart.

(cont'd)

Matron and muse, unhealthily idoled,
lied to and cheated on, saddled and bridled.
Put on a pedestal, yet rarely protected,
ghosted, ignored, destroyed then resurrected,
embarrassed, belittled, sometimes respected.
I've been loved and honoured but still disconnected.
Never a taste of love unconditional,
desperately wanting a life more traditional.

Yes, I've been many things to many men,
but never Daddy's girl.

Missing Champion

When you rise, I doubt
I'm the first thing on your mind.
You pervade my sleep
and waking hours;
you are always on mine.

You drive me to distraction,
turn me inside out, it's true.
I despise that I feel weak,
never myself
whenever I'm with you.

Maybe this *is* me,
a girl who's soft and bares her soul.
I've given out my heart;
please give it back.
Who will fill this hole,

this monstrous, gaping void
that exists within my chest?
Where is my brave, true champion
who thinks I'm worthy of conquest?

He is just a myth, a legend,
though I wish that he were you.
I wonder if you feel at all—
you're like a chiselled stone statue.

(cont'd)

I hope that I am wrong
and love that you are strong,
but I can't tell
if you're hardened to the bone
or if this is just your outer shell.

I've heard that icy hearts can melt
when warmed by passion's flame,
but for that to work, it's not just one,
two hearts must feel the same.

I know not what's on your mind,
can only judge that which I see,
and though your touch is hot,
your gaze is not—
it's like you don't see me.

Brave, I turn, unsheathe my sword,
for now, I defend myself
'til a champion who looks beyond
rescues me from off the shelf.

It's You

The saying goes, *it's not you,*
it's me. You crazy bitch.
I love you. Let's move in together.
Ah, screw it—let's get hitched.

In actual fact, this isn't working.
See you later. Ciao. Goodbye.
Then, it's not right to text you that;
let's say this eye-to-eye.

A shy hello with weak embrace,
a kiss—but we're just friends.
In productive and honest conversation,
we decide to make amends.

The next few days: a fairy tale.
Yes, love, indeed, is blind.
We don't see pain sneaking up,
ready to strike us from behind.

Again, we're at this juncture,
yet for once, I see the truth.
Through teary eyes, I raise my voice:
it isn't me—it's you.

The Game

Why did you give me your number?
I was happy on my own,
with no one to think of calling.
Now, I'm staring at my phone.

I'm waiting for a message
I know will never come.
But wait—*beep beep*—a text from you?
Nope, it's just my alarm.

I never thought you were my type;
I had never considered you
'til you noticed me and took that step—
I wondered what to do.

We talked a bit, and then it came—
a hook-up late one night.
I should've listened to my instincts—
I knew that I was right.

Thanks again for the reminder,
for the unwanted history lesson
on how I am only really worthy
of one hot 'n' sweaty session.

The Sometimes Girl

Most nights, I sit and wonder,
trying to understand why
I'm not good enough for always and a day.

Though I know there's no forever,
I want someone to take my hand,
look as though they see me, and say that they will stay.

I don't want a fairy tale;
don't need gifts that money buys.
All I crave is fun, laughter and respect.

I need a mate who is as strong
and as brave as he is wise,
one who understands that to give, is also to get.

Yet I live in darkest shadow,
where the naked eye can't see,
in a place where nobody can hear a sound.

Alone and bound in silence,
I fall upon my knees,
a pool of tears growing ever deeper on the ground.

In these moments, when my mind
holds only doubt and rage and pain,
when my reflection in the mirror hates itself,

I battle hard to find a reason
why this earth I should not stain
red with blood, and end this sorrow for myself.

(cont'd)

From somewhere deep and desperate,
my soul reaches out and cries,
throws a flare into the darkness and alights

a tiny flicker of a flame
inside my heart before it dies,
so my passion for a contest reignites.

I must do this once again,
convince *myself* that I am worth
something to someone when it always ends this way:

bereft and left to wonder
why I was put here on this earth,
to be the always-sometimes girl, forever cast away.

I Miss You

I miss you.
Like the desert misses rain that never comes.
Like a soldier yearns for those waiting back home.
Like a veiled cavern longing for the sun.
Like a baby that never wants to be alone.

I wish you thought about me in your own time, but you don't.
I wish you wondered if I felt the same.
I wish you could see me as I am, but I know you won't.
All you see are reasons why this is a game.

I know you lie to me, trying to make me feel at ease,
thinking I'll forget that you are still a single man.
I know you give yourself away to others as you please,
and I know I'm not good enough to make your life's grand plan.

So, I hate you.
Like a chastised child scorns a scolding mum and dad.
Like the elderly despise their wasted youth.
Like the time together we never get to have.
Like the lies I tell myself just to avoid the truth.

I still miss you.

Seductive Steel

There it is, that shiny thing,
with edges sharp and true
that glimmer in the moonlight,
lustre of silver, white, and blue.

It tempts me with its offer.
Go on, nullify your pain.
Thrust me deep into that monster
until that bloody beast is slain.

Slice me gently over skin
virgin to the cold of steel.
It stings at first, but then warmth
is all that you will feel.

I watch as it shimmers,
calling out to me.
Maybe this is how it ends.
Perhaps this is my destiny.

Such a stunning contradiction,
this simple little knife—
in one hand, man's own saviour,
in the other, taker of life.

The Wrong Idea

Kiss me, but not with passion.
Keep it distant. Keep it cold.
Don't whisper little nice things in my ear.

Don't caress my face.
Never look deep into my eyes,
or else I might just get the wrong idea.

Please ignore my texts and calls,
at least answer days delayed.
Avoid impressions you're glad to hear from me.

No kiss. No hug. No hello, please.
Smack my ass to say goodbye.
No sign of feelings or emotions should I ever see.

When our bodies meet in passion,
be rough and throw me around,
make me do the things that nice girls never do.

Treat me just the way you want to.
Never ask if I'm okay—
after all, I'll never matter as much as you.

Don't embrace me softly after.
Leave before the sweat is dry.
Whisper something demeaning, cruel, and certainly sleazy.

Recount the things we did together,
forgetting it was also you
passing judgement that I'm just too cheap and easy.

(cont'd)

Allow me time to overthink
before reaching out again.
Use me up and leave me wondering why.

Then drop a line like, *Hey, how are you?*
I really miss you. We should catch up.
Make it look as though you care enough to try.

Don't forget to cancel plans
at the last minute for effect.
Dangle the carrot just to keep me hanging on.

Please try to make me feel
like I'm a psycho and a stalker
for contacting you again after so long.

Please accept my gifts and time
and feign your gratitude.
Never give a single thing back, for I fear

just a simple act of kindness,
a single word misconstrued,
might make me think you give a fuck—
and I know that's the wrong idea.

Regretful

I'm sorry I wasn't strong enough
to wait for you,
that I couldn't put aside my aching heart.

Sorry I wasn't in control of my fears;
I was afraid that, once again,
I'd be left lonely in the dark.

When I look at you, I see your soul
shining like brilliant gold.
My heart feels you're a loyal and honest man.

When you touch me, with your hands or words,
you warm me to my core.
Your smile delves into places nothing else can.

For just a second, you made me think
I'm worthy of a boundless love
and a trust that is as real as it is shared.

I suppose that's why I doubted,
why I faltered, and I ran;
it simply couldn't be true—I was too scared.

Now, I must live with my decision,
my fear, remembering that message,
knowing it's one that I will always regret.

(cont'd)

Still, I hope that I am someone
you will call upon, even if only in dreams.
Here's to our brief encounter—
one I know you won't soon forget.

Thinking of You

My thoughts play out now only in dreams:

small handfuls of your hair pulled tight.
Hot breath through lisping teeth and tongue.
Neck arched, exposed for mouth's delight.

Nails dragged softly down your back, you writhe;
our bodies now moving as one.
Hearts racing, skin flushed— this is to feel alive.

Our eyes meet in tenderness, a perfect look upon your face.
Our bodies pause to hold the deep,
clasped tight, no room for light or space.

Warm moments lose themselves to fire,
and in an almost primal drive of lust,
our pulses rise to match the tempo of desire.

Crescendo building, the rush forms to a peak,
and like an ocean wave growing before the crash,
we break upon each other's shore, fall into arms and sleep.

Though you are no longer here, your scent/your trace still lingers.
My mouth remembers how you taste.
I still feel your hands entwined around my fingers.

Only the Walls

Who was that wicked girl last night,
and whither did she go?
There are traces of her on my sheets,
smudged across lilac pillows.

Flashes of her dance through my head,
a half-remembered, loud-laughing dream.
She tricked me, teased me, and lured him
into my home, into my bed.

With only the walls as witness
to explain the mess that has been made,
I have questions but no answers.
She is gone, and yet he stayed.

Quickly stripped-off evidence
lies strewn across the floor.
My foggy spell bursts with reality—
I can't deny it anymore.

From our unresting drunken stupor,
we slowly start to awake.
My heart sinks in realisation;
that wicked girl was my mistake.

His face now silently speaking,
once again, I've been deceived.
Another piece of me departs in tandem,
      through the doorway, as he leaves…

Apologetic

I'm sorry I love you,
knowing you don't feel the same.

I'm sorry my heart does backflips
whenever I hear your name.

I'm sorry I told you
you're significant (it's true),

I'm sorry I can't retract
all the things I said to you.

I apologise for caring,
for showing glimpses of my heart,

I am sorry for my honesty,
for being upfront from the start.

I apologise for being weak,
for letting you deep inside.

I'm sorry my affection grows,
but now I must confide:

I am sorry I'm not everything
a man desires to keep,

but I'll imagine that you love me
while you hold me as we sleep.

At Arm's Length

I'm strong and yet not quite enough
to fight conviction's strength,
and your decision to not let me close,
to keep me at arm's length.

Though you hold me close to skin at times,
your heart is locked away.
I guess there are little parts of you
still yearning for yesterday.

I'm guilty, too, of building walls
that even you cannot scale,
wondering why you never noticed,
never saw the *me* behind this veil.

I thought that I was honest;
never once did I lie to you.
I suffocate myself, pretending,
denying what is true.

And even if I'm perfect,
if our souls faultlessly intertwine,
you aren't ready to risk your freedom;
if you don't seek, you shall not find.

My heart seeks not to claim you—
I don't need to make you mine.
Just want to be the thought that lights you up,
jumps in your head from time to time.

(cont'd)

I want to be the one you long for
when you are lonely in your bed,
the woman who would 'get' the joke,
knowing your words before they're said.

I'd love to be the lucky one
who greets you when you're home,
the happy voice from far away
when talking on the phone.

The girl who cooks your favourite meal,
loves your weakness and your strength,
but I'm held too far away to try—
I'm just the girl held at arm's length.

If I Were Pretty

In the darker hours, when I'm alone,
still, for a rare moment or two,
I ponder: if I were pretty, would you notice?
Would I be worth a second glance from you?

If I were pretty, would I be of interest,
perhaps a candidate for you to vet?
If I were pretty, would you feel this connection?
I thought I felt your soul the first time we met.

If I were pretty, could I be considered
as more than just a friend?
If I were pretty, would you strike up a conversation,
then not want our encounter to come to an end?

If I were pretty, would you see beneath the surface,
past the flaws and beyond the scars?
But no, I know I'm not your kind of pretty—
so in darker hours, I wish for pretty upon the stars.

Smo

I wish height were infinite.
No roof, no top,—you
lift me up so high,
I'm scared of ever coming down.
I'd climb any mountain and
risk the long and painful drop
to feel this real sensation I've found.

In you, I see the world anew.
There's nothing I wouldn't do
to catch a glimpse of life
through your vivid eyes,
devoid of fears that bend and
skew reality and turn it into lies.

You light me up with your touch,
devouring every part of my flesh.
I'd do anything for the rush of
our bodies melding like mesh.
I'm no fool; I'm smarter now.
Experience has taught me how
to test water before jumping in too deep.

At night, my mind will not allow
my thoughts to rest
or just slow down.
Tell me,
Is it only me who cannot sleep?

(cont'd)

I wish you thought of me the same
way I think of you. It's lame,
I know, but the truth so often is.
Even though this is just a game
for you, perhaps another name
to add to your collection—so be it.

I'll savour every bit of time
I get to spend with you. It's fine;
I think I know how
this will work out anyway.

So, if you need a heart,
take mine,
at least for now,
until you find someone who
makes you feel
the same in every way.

In Memory: Daniel Fox

Who decides which souls to take?
What gives them the right?
They got it so completely wrong
when they chose him last night.

Don't they know we need him here?
His strong but gentle way?
Don't they know they messed shit up
when they took him away?

Can't they see we need his smile,
his laughter and his swag?
They should have let him stay and fight
and one day be a dad.

They should have known his friends
would lose a piece of their hearts,
that his family would feel as though
their world had been torn apart.

It makes no sense to any of us;
there is no explanation why.
There cannot be a reason
that could ever justify.

Unless we pause to wonder
if perhaps a deal was made by *them*.
For a baby born somewhere today,
one pure soul was sent to heaven.

Selfie

We post the selfies and wonder why
the likes don't satisfy
the need to feel noticed and wanted,
never simply glorified.

Our lust is not physicality alone,
but a desire to be seen
and appreciated from the inside.

Your Pretty Eyes

She might like you from the outside,
but does she see inside the dark?
Do you feel a strong connection?
When you talk, is there a spark?

Does she feel the pain inside you?
Can she soothe your restless soul?
Do you touch and melt together,
so that two become one whole?

Does she hold you close for comfort,
squeeze your neck, caress your face?
Will she stand with you in hard times,
give you her strength and all her faith?

Will she scare you with her honesty?
Love the black that most despise?
Will she ever see past the shoreline
to swim the depths of your pretty eyes?

Realisation

Don't speak. Don't say a word.
There is nothing left to say.
Your words won't be heard;
actions speak louder anyway.

Don't feign to care. You're never there.
Your kind words are all a lie.
I'm kept on the bench as a spare
'til a dull moment passes by.

You call to fill in time, and
like always, I'm there for you,
playing tough, pretending it's fine
for you to use me like you do.

But, deep inside my skin,
I'm hurt and ashamed
of the lust I hold within,
of the beast that can't be tamed.

It's not just you, nor only I
that causes all my pain.
And in an attempt to justify,
I repeat the behaviour yet again.

Things from the past come back here,
affecting that which happens now.
History is my greatest fear;
I'd stop it dead if I knew how.

(cont'd)

And yet I know deep inside,
to find answers, I must look within.
Now I see that although I hide
it from myself, I mean naught to him.

I'm just a vessel, a sometimes muse,
not a mate, not even a lover.
Someone he knows will never refuse
despite the presence of another.

And so, perhaps now is the time
for this adultery to come to an end.
I know you'll never be all mine,
so goodbye, my fucking friend.

For Marshall

When I look into your eyes,
my fears are vanquished in the fire
that burns inside your mind,
your soul, your heart.

And yeah, you make me feel invincible.
Your words sure inspire me
to be stronger, tougher and
braver 'spite the past.

I just want you to notice me,
to let me hold you tight.
For you, I'd fight to show you
how these colours can be true.

Those other bitches better watch out
cos I'll knock out all their lights
for every shitty little thing
they've done to you.

I know I'll never catch your eye;
not so pretty you could die.
No massive rack, no
designer clothes, no platinum vagina,

but I'm the best you've yet to meet,
so, at least I have to try
to make you see and admire
that my integrity is finer.

(cont'd)

See, I'm a fighter; yes, I am,
and if you ask me, I will prove it.
I will battle 'til my blood
runs across the whole damn floor.

If you like dancers, play the music;
I can shake it, make you lose it,
and you'll want to take me
right here on the floor.

If you want nasty,
here's your chance;
we can dry hump through your pants
until you rip my panties off so we can play.

If you need loving, I'll bring romance.
What we do's of no importance.
I will show you how
I love you every day.

I digress; I'm not obsessed
with simply getting you undressed.
Truth be told,
I really want to look into

your soul for just a second
to see if, as I guessed,
we're much the same on further insight,
me and you.

(cont'd)

Same as you— oh, I've been screwed,
cheated on more than a time or two.
Matter of fact,
it seems to happen all the time.

Though, I'm not quittin', not givin' up,
no siree, no fucking Bob.
Sometimes love is late
like Toto says in *Hold the Line*.

But shit is better late than never.
Never can fuck itself forever
if never means we'll never
get a chance to meet.

What's that you say? You think I'm boring?
And what's that noise? Is that you snoring?
Go fuck yourself!
You don't know me or who I am.

I guess all that 'don't judge me' shit
you spit ain't really that legit,
or maybe just reserved for you
and Eminem, untouchable misfit.

I s'pose you think I want your money?
Well, go suck your own dick, Honey.
Oh, poor baby,
is it big enough to reach?

(cont'd)

Maybe you should have got to know me
before you said, 'Girl, you can blow me.'
You hypocrite! Make me feel like shit!
Why don't you practice what you preach?

Whoa now! Where the fuck did that come from?
I don't know!
Sometimes shit just comes out all wrong.
This poem's not panning out like I had planned.

You know this rhyming shit ain't easy,
and yes, my experience is measly.
Looks like I blew my one shot,
but I'll be damned.

Now, I'm feeling like a psycho
and a little like a stalker.
No! Please stop! Don't go away!
Boy, give me a break.

All I really want is to know ya,
to be someone you can talk to.
I'm not lying. Not a player.
I'm not a fake.

Now, I'm feeling quite embarrassed,
as I never meant to harass
or annoy you,
and you're probably wondering why

(cont'd)

I would try to write in lyric
and appeal to Marshall Mathers,
but in case none of that matters,
my name is Kylie, spelt

K-I-L-E-Y.

Oh, and I would love to cook you dinner.
Here's my number,
take my digits.
Remember, you can call me on the fly.

Secrets

Insomnia

Another night turns to dawn;
my eyes close,
devoid of sleep.

Tears inside my soul,
a heavy heart—
I must not weep.

Mind spinning, churning,
digging and yearning.
Discombobulated—I feel ill.

Mind erratic, thoughts sporadic.
What the fuck?
Please, just be still.

I want to dig my hands
inside my chest
to rip out my heart,

but I can't, as it's
shredded to pieces,
completely torn apart.

Cut my skin,
let the anger drain,
surround me like a moat.

I want to shout,
but I'm constricted, as though
there are hands around my throat.

(cont'd)

I can't breathe.
Suffocating, reaching
outwardly, I gasp.

I paw the air
to find nothing there—
nothing or no one to grasp.

Feels like I'm failing.
I'm falling
ever deeper, down so low.

There's no returning
from this point,
not from where I'm about to go.

The darkness pulls my hair;
it slaps my face.
I wake with a scream.

Drenched in sweat,
the realisation hits:
life is a nightmare, not a dream.

Little Too Late

How is it even possible,
in one single lonely week,
your whole life comes down to nothing,
with the future looking bleak?

Everything you've worked for
drifts away before your eyes.
The blood, sweat and tears
harden solid as they dry.

Standing like a monument
to all you've sacrificed,
that statue ain't worth nothing,
for with art, there is no price

until the artist isn't breathing,
isn't living anymore.
Seems what you do is of no value
'til you can't do it anymore.

And in your final instant,
when you draw your last short breath,
they'll gasp and act surprised,
suddenly mournful of your death.

The irony is that it's too late,
but now they finally know
you were always worth something,
and they should've told you so.

Social Anxiety

Don't shine too bright, or they'll notice you.
Then they'll be watching, and what will you do?
We can't let them see inside, or they'll know.
They will look too deeply,
see through the facade, and
discover it's all for show.

Perhaps they'll question what you've been ignoring.
We can't appear daft or, worse still, boring.
Neither can we come across as too strong,
for next comes the judgement,
inevitable confrontations,
presumptions we're always wrong.

Don't speak too loudly. Don't take up too much space.
Avoid drawing attention. Try to act with some grace.
Don't be too boisterous, lest seemingly rude.
Laugh politely at crass jokes,
hide your embarrassment,
and keep responses short and subdued.

Perhaps you might meet someone. There's always a chance.
Don't be a wallflower now; go on, have a dance.
But don't get too comfortable. Mind what you're drinking;
we can't have you acting yourself.
Stop talking; he might hurt you.
What the hell are you thinking?

(cont'd)

Don't stay out too long; nothing good happens late.
Make excuses to leave. Accept this is your fate.
Don't stop to think. From these feelings, you must hide.
I can't let you notice the truth and leave us.
We are all the same;
everyone's struggling on the inside.

You Had to Know

Perhaps you didn't mean it
when you stole my trust from me,
but you had to know it hurt.
Shifting blame made me feel guilty.

Your hands said more than mouths
could ever say without a sound;
grabbed me like a butcher does a carcass,
with little force, you held me down.

Through teary eyes, I looked up at you,
your demented, twisted face;
it looked as though your pleasure
came devoid of all disgrace.

As I cried, you moaned.
I kicked in vain and hit your grotesque head.
I tried to summon up a demon,
pleaded for death to meet me in that bed.

And though you never struck me,
I wish to hell you did,
for at least I'd have felt something other
than your sick lust and dark hatred.

Worse still, the times I woke
to find my choice taken away,
any ounce of pride or power stolen;
guess I never had any anyway.

(cont'd)

Never once did you apologise.
Instead, you had the bloody nerve
to make me feel it was all my fault,
that this abuse was what I deserved.

Now it's over, at least for you,
though, in my heart, I still feel lost.
I wonder if the prize you won
was worth my lifelong cost.

Left loaded with this damage,
desperately wishing it wasn't so,
my rage still questions why you did it.
I'm sure you had to know.

Submission

Close your eyes and touch me, please,
I beg you.
It's dark, so don't worry;
tonight, I can be
whoever you want me to be.

Lay back, Baby, and dream.
Am I bad? Can I scream?

Do you want me rough and dirty?
Would you prefer I just submit?
Tell me how you want it done,
how you feel and that you want it.

Do I suck?
Do I swallow? Do I bite?

What do I have to do
to make you want me on this night?
I can see it in your eyes and
feel it deep within my core.
You want more, you
self-absorbed whore.

Grab me roughly with desperate hands,
by the waist or by the hair.

(cont'd)

Never mind that you hate me.
Forget the fact that you don't care.
Tonight, I'll get my share.
You need me now; that's all that counts.
I'm here to satisfy your every need,
thinking nothing of my own.

Use me. Abuse me.
Fornicate me.

Treat me like the object I need to be
to get through this night so that for a moment
I won't be lonely.
Pull my hair, slap my face, disregard my tears.
Do whatever you need to do to realise your deepest, darkest fears—

then leave
before the lust-coloured tint wears off.

Leave before you realise
the mistake you've made,

before you start to hate me
for everything you asked me to be.
Tear me down, push me aside.
I'm nothing but a free and easy ride.

Don't try to hide your lack of respect;
if you held any at all,

(cont'd)

you wouldn't have touched me that way.
Not that it matters. I'll never see you again.
I'll ask you to leave, because I know
you'll never stay.

Spare me the speech,
the kiss goodbye and the promises.
Submission always ends the same way.

Does She Know?

I watch as you touch her.
I'm not jealous;
I am scared,
remembering that feeling inside my skin.

In those last moments, the ending,
your insistence
despite my tears.
You punched holes into my walls so paper-thin.

Does she know that side of you?
The blackest rage?
Forceless oppression?
How you stripped me down to nothing but a shell?

You have a face for others,
just for show,
to convince yourself
your spirituality could come from raising hell.

How dare you be so happy!
It's not right.
I'm so alone—
why should you be allowed to wear a smile?

You profess your love for her to me,
play out your perfect life,
watching me sacrifice and
struggle through this web of pure defile.

(cont'd)

I hate your face, your voice, your games,
your twisted versions of truth.
I despise your many deceptive tales
and resent the fact that I feel like I lost.

My lessons learned have earned *you* this;
a second chance with someone else.
But does she know that her happiness
came entirely at my cost?

Black Angel

She flew
on blackened wings of dragon flame,
her softness fallen
to screams of rage and pain.

Strong in embrace, not of hate or love,
she clung with vengeance to my soul.
I felt doomed, in fear of a fate
that I'd be buried alive in this black hole.

In disgrace, she cast me downward,
the bitch caring naught about my tears.
She suffocated what light remained
and brought forward all my fears.

Defiant, although beaten,
I lashed out, desperate to flee.
I smashed and slashed, destroying her image,
my flesh not even worth a pound for free.

My bleeding hands clung to the evidence,
a shattered mirror in which I could see
the bitch that hurts and cuts at my feelings—
she is, and always was, me.

Drunk

Disconnected

from it all.
From everyone.

Is it me?
It's my way
to be alone.
To wander.

Nowhere is where
I belong.
Not a standout, never mingle,
just another lone female.

Not flashy, not a single
white glove like Michael's.
I'm no hallmark—
not even a calling card.

It's a cycle…

Round it goes, and
here I am again,
sick of it.
I just want it all to end.

Maybe tonight.
Will I fight?

(cont'd)

Seriously, I'm done.
Let me come undone;
it's all I want to do.

Unstick the tiny pieces,
the opposite of glue.

You can find me
at the bottom,
deep below
the surface.

There's no purpose
in your talking.
I can't hear, and honestly,
I don't care what you're saying.

There's no point in yelling
or whispering stories in my ear.
Zero fucks is all I'll give—
my gift to you for free.

No matter.
You don't notice
this small heart, my mind,
or me.

Crawling

Hurt me gently.
Lick my wounds.
Choke me from behind,
then softly spoon.
Please just be the man I need right now.

Dig your fingers
deep into my soul.
Squeeze me so hard
my pieces come back whole.
Please just be the man I need right now.

Whisper painful truths
into my ears.
Say you will stay.
With your brow, wipe my tears.
Please just be the man I need right now.

Caress my dark;
let me lighten yours.
Don't promise me tomorrow.
I'm crawling on all fours.
Please, just be the man I need right now.

Matriarchy

I don't want to wear this name
laden with such guilt and shame.
No longer good,
no longer golden,
I am the child you had no hold on.

You drove it to this awful place,
spitting venom in my face.
My reaction?
What could I do?
Not fucking weak and scared, like you.

Screamed insults and pointed fingers,
words forgotten, though anger lingers.
With no more love
inside to give,
a shallow life you must now live.

Don't blame the past for your behaviour—
eternal victim, no power, no saviour.
You made them turn their backs on me.
Their ears didn't hear,
so their eyes won't see.

Stay over there and hide the lies,
burying them under the truth you despise.
I never hurt you,
though, lord knows, I could;
you tried to push me so I would.

(cont'd)

Then you'd have someone you could blame,
instead of dealing with all your shame.
I'm unsure why you hate me,
but this fact I know is true:
I'll live my life trying *not* to be you.

2015

Distended belly
full of hate,
with rage spawned from shame.
Cut my face,
spite your attraction.
Now go on, say again, I'm vain.

Now, she's standing
right beside you,
unaware of what's in store.
I hear you laugh
as you verbally dismember
parts of her onto the floor.

To the Bone

Deeper than knife,
sharper than blade,
ever wider has the wound been made
by tongue and truth alone.

Bright red flesh
'neath stinging skin
cut through by turn of phrase.
No blood, just pain and sorrow to the bone.

Amanda

Crank the handle tighter.
The black claws strangle the last living breath of hope.
I feel them tight around my soul.
Why do they cling so fervently?
There is nothing left to take.
Shut up and stop crying.

Sobs fall on the ears of an empty room.
Tears shed in vain but still they flow,
their warmth the only comfort in this lonely world.
My head aches and my body hurts.
What is this pain in my belly, and why won't it go?

Tomorrow should be better, but it never is.
I wish I had the answers, but the more I search,
the more questions and anguish I conjure.
I wonder, is this how you felt, Amanda?

Reclamation

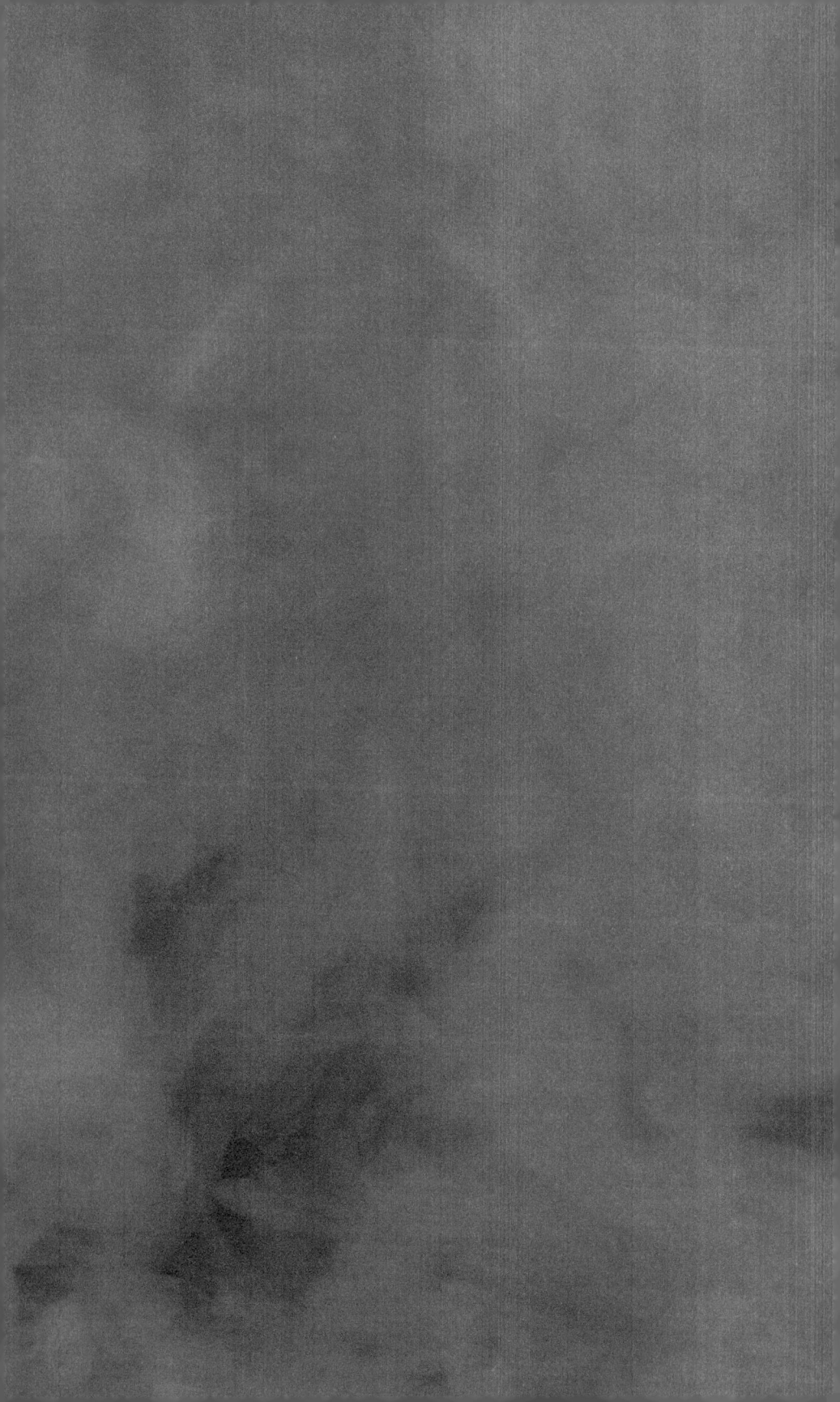

Liar Liar

How dare you try to push me
down so low.
I won't go,
won't let you take my life away from me.

You will not win this battle.
I don't think so!
I know I am stronger than before,
and now you'll see,

despite the knife that's in my hand,
my cut skin,
the pain I'm in.
The pain is nothing that I haven't felt before.

Last time you didn't kill me;
you did not win.
I was the king,
a soldier, slaying enemies at my door.

You think you have me beat,
but you are wrong.
I am strong,
and there's nothing you can take
when there's nothing left to give.

All I have is my will,
but I'm not sharing.

(cont'd)

I'll fight long,
my word is bond.
Nothing's as powerful as
one's own will to live.

So, step aside
and let me move forward.
Take your bow;
this shit stops now!
Don't even think you have a chance
to end this fight.

I've been training, and I'm ready
for this bout,
and I'll leave you wondering how
you'll walk away
and ever live after tonight.

It's not my plan to vanquish,
just to make you go away.
You cannot stay.
The gods already have a plan
for your death.

But it dawns—
the gods also planned for me.
On this day,
I'll fade away,
everything just a lie,
leaving you with my last breath…

Fighting

Heart beating loudly in my ears,
almost bursting through my chest.
The time is now to test and see
who wins and who is best.

It's down to just the two of us.
We're standing toe to toe.
Have I trained enough for this?
Well, soon we shall all know.

Doubt creeps inside my mind.
Its suspicion almost hurts.
My body turns to jelly, then to numb;
uncertain which is worse.

I try to psyche myself back up,
but it's as though there is no use.
Still, there's no backing out of this,
no possible treaty, pact or truce.

I turn my mind inside to
remember why I'm here.
From somewhere deep, it rises—
a thunderous roaring in my ears,

like a lion in the jungle
or a band of Samurai,
emerging through forests thick,
bellowing battle cries.

(cont'd)

Perhaps the crowd is all I hear,
but I'm sure it's something else.
That rumble is how it sounds
when defeating fear itself.

Now, adrenaline is pumping,
the room shrinks down in size.
I'm at one end of a tunnel;
at the other end is my prize.

This prize is not a trophy,
no, not a piece of tin.
It's justice, pride and respect I seek—
the reward, not merely the win.

The Dojo

Here I stand,
delivered unto you,
ready to be stripped bare,
broken down and torn apart,
with no questions remaining there.

Drive me to the ground.
No easy task. I've been before.
I've given you my all,
yet still you push,
demanding more.

Sweat pours from my body—
out of every single pore.
It feels like life is draining
out of my soul and
onto the floor.

At some point in the night,
I wonder what I came here for.
Then you hit me
and kick me with a force
that makes me tremble to my core.

Mixed emotions,
both love and hatred
for the things you do to me,
for the way you make me feel;
blind, but now I see.

(cont'd)

When my world outside's
in turmoil and
makes me feel crazy,
everything makes sense with you,
my dojo,
my dōgi.

The Dragon Within

Inside me lives a dragon,
fierce, strong, and true.
It strikes my words to burn like fire
and light up the truth in you.

There is nothing you can do
to stop the beast once it's unleashed.
Can't take back your words or deeds now done.

But you'll regret your shallow actions
when I rip out your heart and devour it.
You took mine and don't need *yet* another one.

Once I have crushed you,
I'll roar, causing all below to tremble,
rage rising in my widened, blood-red eyes.

Watch me fly away,
swirling above and all around you.
There are greater things for me beyond your skies.

Now I am gone, but you must stay,
nothing but an ember.
Remember how you thought me simply meek and mild?

You thought you had me wrapped tight
around your tiny, little finger,
forgetting I'm an adult, not a child.

(cont'd)

Inside me lives a dragon,
fierce, strong, and true.
Sleeping now but always present,
it keeps watch for men like you.

Namaste

Heat surrounds me,
warming me from the inside.
I know that in this room,
there is nowhere I can hide.

Not from them, nor from myself;
my true nature will be revealed.
Weakness shall be forged to strength.
My wounds, through pain, will heal.

Though I may struggle, even falter—
some days, perhaps, even fail—
persevere I shall,
so in the end, I will prevail.

My mind will sometimes panic,
and at times, I'll doubt myself,
but if I relax and remember to breathe,
I know thy body knows itself.

I trust the path, the postures,
and I honour myself today.
Savasana is not the space between,
but the way I live each day.

Let it Fall

Mother Earth beneath me,
face upturned to the sky,
raindrops fall like tears upon my face,
each icy droplet waking me
from despair.

I am comforted in knowing
the discomfort of cold,
and in distraction from the
gripping pain and angst,
I send a wish for the night to take me.

Take me behind the veil
of tightly shut eyelids
where I can allow myself to dream,
and no shadow can be cast
from my bright, loving light.

Let the rain fall and wash away the past,
leaving naked skin to cover
newborn flesh.
May the water flow and
cleanse my heart of hurt and censure.

But in the dawn of opened eyes,
I return to my nightmare,
forced to view the mirror of my soul,
an ugly truth revealed
to all in open sight.

At the rise of a new tomorrow,
as the sun splits dark from light,
I plead the solar rays burn what has washed away,
to leave incinerated
the charred remains of the old me.

What If?

If there was no tomorrow,
how would you choose to live today?

If now was your last moment
with loved ones, what would you say?

Don't look back, but pause to think
about your journey up until now.

Is there something you must do before
time's gun is on your brow?

Before the bell has rung, the Reaper's come,
and darkness turns to night.

What is left burning in your chest?
That thing you wish was I *will*, not I *might*.

What is the fear that grips you and
stops you still when you should go?

Life's purpose is to find our gift,
to give it and to grow.

Out of Shadow

The passing dark is full of shadows,
with occasional windows of light.
My heavy breath is visible in the cold air.
The balls of my feet land quickly on the ground,
pushing me ever further into the night.

I turn to look behind me.
At this speed, my vision fails.
A grip in my chest tightens,
forcing a struggle for each breath.
My eyes water,
wide black pupils covered in teary veils.

Heartbeat racing, sweat dripping,
the distance draws ever near.
I will my legs to forge on faster
and remove me from those voices.
Flee me to safety
lest I meet the one I fear.

As I run, I feel I'm fading.
Where is the strength I had before?
I want that fire back,
that burning energy,
not the here-now panic in my veins.
It is in me somewhere, buried deep within my core.

(cont'd)

The path before me starts to blur;
scenery distorts before my eyes.
In confusion, my legs falter beneath me.
I hit the pavement like a drunkard,
blood edging down my face,
but disorderly, I rise

like a slow-dawning day.
When nightfall parts to rays of sun,
I pause,
my spinning head slows to clarity,
and I see my past behind
and learn it's from myself I run.

An understanding sweeps my conscience,
as though I know what life's about.
Despite my flaws,
failures, and imagined fears,
if I'm to ever stand in sunlight,
I must escape lingering shadows of self-doubt.

Cracks

The cracks are on the inside—
in case you didn't know—
covered with smiles and laughter,
so the wounds, they cannot show.

The cracks are growing deeper,
though they no longer bleed.
They allow the pain to penetrate,
and on my fears they feed.

The cracks cannot be mended
by application of another.
My worthiness will not be measured
in my value to a lover.

The cracks begin to surface
despite attempts to run and hide,
but I've earned each crack, each battle scar,
so, like medals, I wear them all with pride.

Spinning Cranes

Spent and drenched in sweat,
I look up at spinning cranes.
My flaccid arms weigh heavy.
Hearing the creaking chains,
I remind myself that this is life—
here is where I heal my pain.

It matters not that you don't care,
deaf to hear me scream.
I push far beyond the pain you caused,
past the knife and its tempting gleam.
Its beautiful sting will not entice me,
not while I dare to dream.

Forgive Me

I long to give forgiveness,
lay sins of the past to rest.
To feel the weight of nothingness,
and rid this burden from my chest.

Each day, there are reminders—
words that echo in my ears.
My failures prove that you were right
and give power to all my fears.

If I could wash away the memories,
clear the slate and start anew,
perhaps I'd finally see myself
sans the filter that was you.

So, with strength forged in sufferance,
I resolve to move ahead.
I'll search within to find the reasons
to forgive myself instead.

If

If only we took our own advice,
oh, the lessons we could teach
to ourselves, and likely others,
if we practised what we preach.

Never Give Up

Clouded by judgement,
not of others, but of me.
The smallest things unveil it:
a pebble makes a ripple in the pond,
a wave starts a tsunami in the sea.

Life can alter in an instant.
The only certainty is change.
Though we may not always see it,
things always eventually work out;
in our favour, events will arrange.

The Mighty Queen

Universe, you win this time,
though soldier on I will.
I won't stop until I'm dead
and/or my blood is still.

Another cut to make me bleed,
but I am not stone just yet.
Armour on and sword in hand,
my battle cry is all you'll get.

Come one, come all, but none shall pass;
I've dug my trenches long and deep.
I stand atop every wall,
so now I shall not sleep.

With my victory assured, tales of legend
I know they'll sing,
of how an army could not conquer
this mighty queen without a king.

Ode to a New Year

Don't make empty promises
you don't intend to keep.
Your word is bond;
it is your honour,
it is you.

Words cannot be retracted,
so think before you speak.
Don't be a gossip,
don't be deceitful.
Please, just be true.

Ensure your thoughts are ever positive,
and dare to have a dream.
Your thoughts manifest
the things you hold,
and touch and feel.

Forget self-imposed limitations;
reality is just
what our minds accept
as possible,
and as real.

Accept victory with humility,
and your losses just the same.
To lose is not to fail;
it is to live,
more so, to learn.

(cont'd)

Sometimes, lessons come to us
through our struggles and our pain.
Our strength resolved,
our will iron-forged.
Respect is earned.

Forgive your sins and those of others,
even though you'll not forget.
Live in the present,
not the future,
and never in the past.

Love your lovers, hold your children.
What you give is
what you get.
Remember, life is brief;
and passes so very fast.

Savour every precious moment,
be slow to anger and quick to smile.
Chase your passions,
not possessions—
you already have enough.

Treasure friendships and growing older,
conscious all the while
that it's not wealth
we give and take away with us—
all we truly have is love.

Obsidian

Deep, black volcanic mass, I figured you
magnanimous. I was wrong.
You did exactly as was asked:
reflected parts of me that I needed to see,
then shattered, a broken mirror in fragments,
shards of razor-sharp glass.

I tiptoed over the debris,
scared I'd lose whatever remained.
From the black, red appeared,
a thread of friendship wrapped around my wrist,
held together by thin strings.
Hope sustained.

Despite your insensitivity,
you protected me. All the while,
still broken,
painful and disorientated.
I see now that my shadow lingers,
but the light, it shall never defile.

Accepting there's always polarity:
sometimes, I'll love,
sometimes, I'll fight.
Balance always seeks to exist.
There can never be a shadow cast
without the presence of light.

(cont'd)

When everything escalated under your direction,
though admittedly at my behest,
I stumbled and faltered and almost quit.
The unthinkable occurred.
Digging in the filth, I found the gold
buried deep inside of it.

Like a phoenix from the ashes,
I must seek to rise anew,
but with no way around myself,
I seek to delve inside.
The only possible way out
is to go right through.

So, I ask you now for guidance,
the gifts of truth and mystery.
In the womb of my creation,
I'll be weaving spells of love,
tying together all the loose ends
into a brand-new tapestry.

Acknowledgements

This poetry collection has been brewing for many years, since the time I was a broody teenager sitting in my bedroom with no smart phone, no computer, and just a pen and notebook for company. For the most part I wrote as I found it a way to clear my head, not really having anyone I felt I could really talk to about anything personal. I very much kept my feelings all to myself and was embarrassed to share them.

I regret burning a pile of old poetry during a difficult time in my life, after having kept it for almost twenty years after writing, but I kept envisioning my year 12 English CAT (a small poetry collection) handed back to me with a low grade….and no words of encouragement or advice. I just felt that I couldn't and shouldn't write.

Years later, in a trying time when everything was falling apart it was really Eminem that gave me courage, and it felt like permission to write again. The Poem For Marshall pays homage to that.

I would like to thank my wonderful Editor Krystle for her red edits – and delicately brutal at times suggestions. My poetry has really blossomed under her care, and I've grown considerably through this process. Thankyou for pushing me.

Thanks also go to Les @ Busybird Publishing for pestering me enough about actually doing something with my poems that I did. Thanks for spending too much time trying to find the right font, questioning title choices and front cover suggestions, and helping to make this a book to be proud of. I guess I owe you some Kingston's.

Thanks Busybird Publishing again for being a place of encouragement and opportunity. The monthly open mic nights have been a great space to practice reading my poetry and testing them out on others. We all appreciate our Wed nights and approx. 4 mins on stage, and all the work and time that needs to be given by others for that to happen.

Many thanks to Marcela for taking time out of your busy life to read my collection and offer your very experienced and well-studied perspective. I appreciate that you took it so seriously you almost wrote a thesis – perhaps next time I should be more clear as to what I require upfront ! Seriously however, Thankyou. It means a lot.

Lastly…I don't want to sound like a Christina Aguilera song, but I do want to thank those that hurt me and those times that were difficult. Without those…without the pain and suffering, these poems wouldn't exist. We need the sun, but also the rain to grow.

About the Author

Who is Kiley Baker? Well.... She is her own woman who doesn't like no for an answer but is learning, (still), to accept that sometimes perhaps the universe does know best.

Slowly after many years she is becoming aware that oftentimes a closed door or a failed relationship is a painful and frustrating redirection, but also a savior in ways. It's all a learning process, and that in time and in retrospect, things start to make more sense.

Kiley is a mum of three and the owner and head instructor of her own martial arts academy in Melbourne, Australia. She does not wish to reveal her age, because well only children like to declare that, but has been doing Karate and Kickboxing for over 30 yrs now.

Kiley has too many hobbies (and too much stuff according to her kids and partner) but she does love challenges and trying new things. She likes to try her hand at painting and craft, and at time of printing this collection, she is currently trying to learn to play the violin. Yep.... Kiley is far too busy for her own good, which is why she keeps buying more pot plants to look after and trying to fit in time to keep writing in between.

This is Kiley's fourth published book across four different genres, and she is currently working away on another children's book, and more poetry. You know....in between time. Will she finish them? ...Only the Walls know

At just five years of age, Varley doesn't know why the world has come to a standstill.

He doesn't know why he can't go to school, can't see his friends, and can't go to the park.

He doesn't know why he's stuck at home with Mum and Dad.

All the colour's faded from Varley's life, and he doesn't understand his feelings of confusion, frustration, and anger.

But a chance meeting leads to a glimmer of hope and, with that, the possibility of a whole new outlook.

The Day the Colours Went Away is a poignant exploration of adolescent depression through a child's perspective, and also includes fun and educational activities for kids to do with their teachers at school, or at home with Mum and Dad.

> "... a beautifully written story that takes you back to a once in a lifetime experience when we were able to spend time with our families free from the usual external pressures and commitments."
> – Veronica

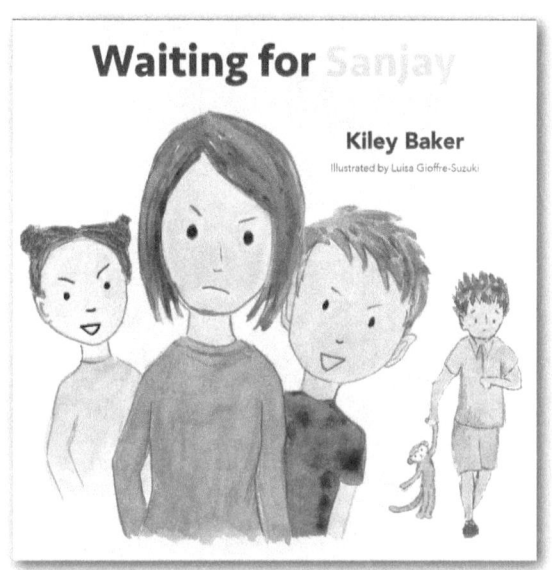

Is Sanjay a naughty boy?

Sanjay loves his teddy and monkey and if given the chance will do parkour on the stairs.

There are so many fun and interesting things all around him that sometimes Sanjay gets distracted and forgets what he should be doing and then everyone is angry with him.

His brother and sister say he's not cool and that upsets him, and then Mum is always yelling at him to hurry up. Sanjay tries to do what Mum tells him but it doesn't always work out the way it should.

Are you like Sanjay?

> "An enjoyable and engaging light-hearted story about everyday challenges of parenting and reflecting life through the eyes of a child. A warm and caring story that will be read again and again."
> – Monique Jarman and Sandy Stockton
> *Kinder teachers with over 20 years' experience.*

Do you feel pressured by the burden of trying to be everything to everyone?

Do you struggle with the task of being a mother to children, a lover to a partner, and a woman true to yourself?

In this raw and honest book, Kiley Baker explains her belief that it takes a warrior to be all of these things.

Mother Lover Woman Warrior examines the art of embracing imperfection and how doing so can empower you to be happier, healthier and achieve so much more out of life.

Sharing from her own life experiences, Kiley presents a practical, easy-to-follow manual that will motivate and change you for the better!

Eltham Martial Arts Academy (Musubi Dojo) offers high-quality martial arts and fitness training in Research, Victoria.

Our programs include Kyokushin Karate, Brazilian Jiu-Jitsu (BJJ), Aikido, Muay Thai Kickboxing, kids martial arts, and women-only Jiu-Jitsu & fitness classes.

We provide structured training for all levels, from beginners to advanced practitioners, helping students build confidence, discipline, and strength.

Join us for a free 7-day trial to experience the benefits of martial arts firsthand.

Our functional fitness training incorporates strength, endurance, and mobility exercises tailored for all ages.

We also offer infrared sauna, remedial massage and ice bath recovery sessions to enhance recovery, reduce muscle soreness, and improve overall well-being.

Where to Find Me ...

www.youtube.com/@Kileybakerauthor

Kileybaker.com

Kiley_baker_author

www.elthammartialarts.com

emaa_musubidojo

www.ingramcontent.com/pod-product-compliance
Lightning Source LLC
Chambersburg PA
CBHW020109240426
43661CB00002B/90